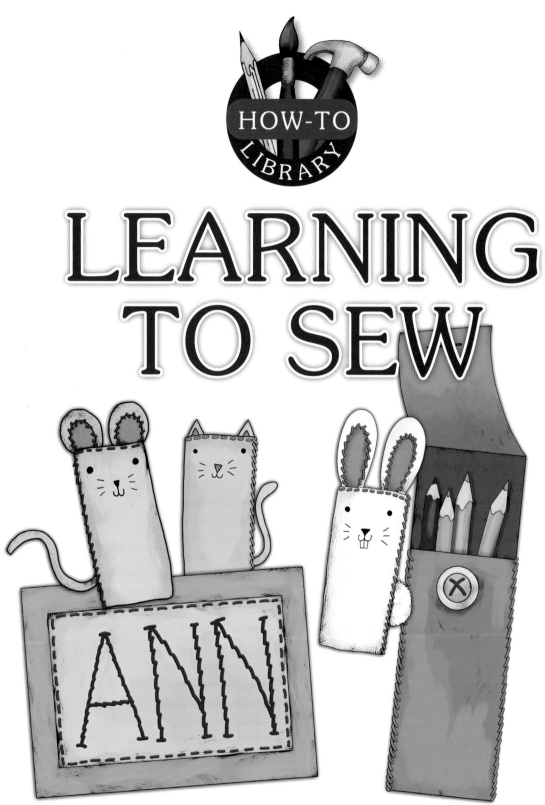

HOW-TO LIBRARY

LEARNING TO SEW

Written and Illustrated by Kathleen Petelinsek

CHERRY LAKE PUBLISHING • ANN ARBOR, MICHIGAN

CHERRY LAKE Publishing

A NOTE TO ADULTS:
Please review the instructions for these craft projects before your children make them. Be sure to help them with any steps you do not think they can safely do on their own.

A NOTE TO KIDS:
Be sure to ask an adult for help with these craft activities when you need it. Always put your safety first!

Published in the United States of America by Cherry Lake Publishing
Ann Arbor, Michigan
www.cherrylakepublishing.com

Photo Credits: Page 4, ©buffaloboy2513/Shutterstock.com; page 5, ©Neveshkin Nikolay/Shutterstock.com; page 6, ©djem/Shutterstock.com; page 7, ©vvoe/Shutterstock.com; page 9, ©Lubava/Shutterstock.com; page 29, ©Jonathan Ross/Dreamstime.com.

Library of Congress Cataloging-in-Publication Data
Petelinsek, Kathleen, author.
  Learning to sew / by Kathleen Petelinsek.
    pages cm. — (Crafts) (How-to library) Includes bibliographical references and index.
  Summary: "Complete a variety of fun sewing projects"
— Provided by publisher.
  Audience: Grades 4 to 6.
  ISBN 978-1-63137-780-8 (lib. bdg.) — ISBN 978-1-63137-800-3 (pbk.)
— ISBN 978-1-63137-840-9 (e-book) — ISBN 978-1-63137-820-1 (pdf)
  1. Sewing—Juvenile literature. 2. Stitches (Sewing)—Juvenile literature.
3. Handicraft—Juvenile literature. I. Title.

  TT712.P48 2014
  646.2—dc23   2014002511

Cherry Lake Publishing would like to acknowledge the work of The Partnership for 21st Century Skills. Please visit www.p21.org for more information.

Printed in the United States of America
Corporate Graphics Inc.
July 2014

TABLE OF CONTENTS

The History of Sewing

At one time, everything was sewn by hand, though that is rare now.

Sewing is the process of fastening things together using stitches. People have been sewing for thousands of years. Ancient people used a basic method of sewing to fasten together skins or furs to make clothing and other items. They used needles made of bone. Their thread was made from animal guts or veins.

People eventually began using fabric and threads similar to the ones still used today. Fabric was once very expensive. People usually mended their torn or worn clothing instead of buying new things to wear. Faded **garments** were turned inside out. When something was too damaged for mending, it was carefully taken apart and made into a new garment or quilt.

This all changed during a time that is now known as the Industrial Revolution. Between the early 1800s and 1860s, factories began to **mass-produce** cotton cloth and thread. This made them cheaper and easier to come by. Most people visited expert **tailors** to have their garments made.

Textile factories began producing fabric cheaply and quickly in the 19th century.

Sewing Revolutionized

Today, sewing machines are common household items.

The first sewing machine was **patented** in 1790. However, using this machine was slower than sewing by hand. In the 1850s, Isaac Singer invented the first sewing machine that surpassed the speed of a seamstress or tailor. **Textile** factories were equipped with the machines, and poorly paid workers used them to mass-produce clothing. Instead of making clothes at home or visiting tailors, people began buying their clothes at stores.

By the 20th century, sewing machines were cheaper and smaller. People began buying them and making their own interesting clothing designs at home. Ebenezer Butterick, an American tailor, created patterns for sewers to follow. Such patterns are widely used today.

By tracing pieces of a pattern and cutting them out, sewers can easily complete even complicated projects.

Your Sewing Basket

You will need to gather some supplies to create the projects in this book. Store them in a basket so they are organized and ready to go whenever you want to sew.

- **Material:** You can sew using many kinds of materials. Some projects use felt. Others use fabric or fleece. Check each project to see exactly what you will need. If you are buying material at a fabric store, a good place to check is the remnant table. This table has small bits of fabric from the end of a fabric roll. It is usually much cheaper than fabric cut fresh from the roll.
- **Needles:** Needles come in a variety of sizes. The sizes are numbered. The higher the number, the smaller the needle. There are also different types of needles. Sharp needles are good for fabric. Embroidery needles are good for felt. They are generally larger than sharp needles. This makes them good for beginners. This book will use both types of needles. The size you should use depends on the type of material and thread you are using.
- **Sewing thread:** An all-purpose cotton thread will work well for most projects in this book. When you use this thread, you will need a sharp needle.
- **Embroidery thread or floss:** This thread is much thicker than cotton thread. It will be used for projects in this book.

It is also a good thread to practice with. You will use an embroidery needle for this thread.

Gather your supplies in a basket to keep them organized.

- **Pins:** Pins are used to hold your fabric in place before you sew it. You can store your pins in a pincushion as you work.
- **Scissors:** Make sure you have a good pair of sharp scissors. The best scissors for sewing projects are called dressmaking shears. Only cut fabric or thread with these scissors. You can make them dull if you use them to cut paper.
- **Tape measure:** This is a flexible ruler. You will use it to measure material before marking and cutting it.
- **Buttons:** You can buy buttons or collect them from old clothing. Start a collection jar of buttons so you have many to choose from when you need them.
- **Water-soluble markers:** You can buy these markers at a fabric store. They are used to mark your fabric. The ink washes off with water.
- **Sewing machine:** Most of the projects in this book do not require a sewing machine. However, a machine is needed for the last two.

Once you have gathered your supplies, you can thread your needle and get started!

Basic Stitches

There are a few basic stitches used in this book. Learning them will start you on the path to becoming an expert tailor! Practice the stitches with a piece of scrap felt or even paper before you stitch your project.

Materials

- Embroidery thread
- Embroidery needle (sizes 1–6 work best)
- Scrap felt or paper
- Scissors

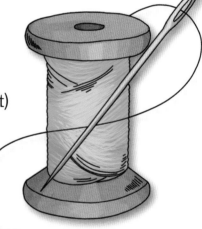

Threading a Needle

Threading a needle is the first step to sewing.

Steps

1. Start by choosing a needle. Needles come in many different sizes. Choose a needle that has an eye large enough that the thread you are using will easily fit through it.
2. Cut your thread to length. Thread longer than 36 inches (91 cm) will tangle easily. If you cut the thread too short, you will run out before you are done. It is easier to rethread a needle than it is to untangle it. Err on the side that is shorter.
3. Insert the thread through the eye of the needle. Hold the needle between your thumb and forefinger and poke the

thread through the eye. If the thread doesn't want
to go through, wet the end of the thread with your mouth.
4. Pull the thread through to meet the other end of the thread
and tie a knot.

Running Stitch

This stitch can be done using one piece of fabric. It can also
be used to sew two pieces of fabric together.

Steps

1. Start by poking your threaded needle from the back of the
fabric up through to the front. Pull the thread all the way
through the fabric.
2. Poke the needle back through the front of the fabric next
to where it just came from. Pull the thread through. You
have created your first stitch!
3. Repeat, leaving a small space between each poke. Try to
follow along a straight line as you stitch.

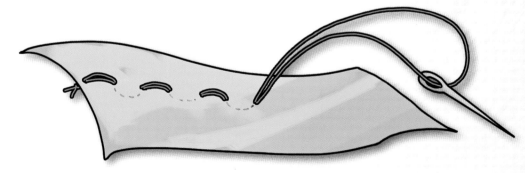

Backstitch

Like the running stitch, the backstitch creates a line made up of straight stitches. However, there is no space between each stitch. This stitch can be used on a single piece of fabric or to sew two pieces of fabric together. It is often used to create decorative designs on items.

Steps

1. Start by poking the needle from the back of the fabric up through the front.
2. Poke the needle back through the front of the fabric next to where it came from. Pull the thread. This is exactly how you started the running stitch.
3. Now poke the needle from the back up through the front next to where it went down through the fabric.
4. This time when you go back down through the fabric, poke the fabric at the end of the first stitch.
5. Keep repeating steps 3 and 4, poking the needle down through the previous stitch each time.

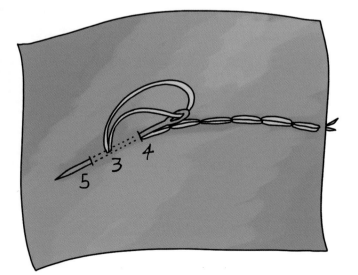

Overcast Stitch

The overcast stitch is used to secure cut edges of fabric so they won't fray. The stitch is done along the edge of the fabric.

Steps

1. Start by poking the needle through both pieces of fabric from the bottom side. Your needle will come out through the top of the fabric. Loop around the edge of the fabric and poke back through the bottom side of the fabric.

2. Repeat step 1 making equally spaced diagonal stitches along the edge of the fabric.

Knot

Whenever you finish stitching, you should knot the end of your thread to keep your project from coming apart.

Steps

1. On the back side of your fabric, form a loop in your thread. Now put your needle through the loop. This will create the beginning of your knot.

2. As you pull the thread with the needle, guide the knot down toward your fabric. You want the knot to lie right next to the last stitch in your fabric. Pull the knot tight.

Initial Sewing Project

This is a great first sewing project. Sew your initials onto a piece of felt and hang it in your room.

Materials

- Tape measure
- Water-soluble marker
- 2 pieces of felt, different colors
- Scissors
- Pins
- Embroidery thread
- Embroidery needle (sizes 1–6 work best)

Steps

1. Use your tape measure to mark a 4 x 6-inch (10 x 15 cm) rectangle with the marker on one of the pieces of felt. Cut carefully along the lines.
2. Measure and mark the second piece of felt with a 3 x 5-inch (8 x 13 cm) rectangle. Cut along the marked lines.
3. Center the smaller rectangle on top of the larger rectangle. Pin the two together to keep them from slipping.

4. Thread your needle and start a running stitch in the corner of your pinned piece. Stitch ¼ inch (0.6 cm) in from the edge of the smaller rectangle to sew the two rectangles together. Continue stitching until you are all the way around the rectangle and back to where you started. Tie a knot on the back of the larger rectangle. You have created a stitched border around your felt. Remove the pins.

5. Use the marker to write your name in block letters on the smaller rectangle.

6. Thread your needle and backstitch along the lines of the letters. Knot your thread as you finish each letter.

7. Wash the marker off your felt. Your name is now stitched into the felt!

Pocket Scarf

This scarf will keep you warm and give you a place to store things at the same time!

Materials
- Fleece (12 x 60 inches, or 30 x 152 cm)
- Measuring tape
- Pins
- Embroidery thread
- Embroidery needle (size 6 works best)
- Water-soluble marker
- Scissors
- 2 large buttons (make sure the needle fits through the holes of the buttons)

Steps
1. Lay your fleece flat on a table. Measure 6 inches (15 cm) from one of the ends and fold the fabric over. Pin it to secure it. Do the same to the other end. This will form a pocket on each end of your scarf.
2. Thread your needle and use the overcast stitch to sew the edges of

the pocket and scarf together. When you get done with one side, knot the thread. Do this to both sides of each pocket. Remove the pins when you are done.

3. On one pocket, measure 1 inch (2.5 cm) down from the top of the pocket. Mark the spot with the marker. Do the same to the other pocket.

4. Use your scissors to cut a small, horizontal slit in the pocket. The slit should be about as wide as the **diameter** of your button. Be careful not to cut the bottom side of the scarf. Only cut the pocket. Do this to both pockets.

5. Use the marker to mark the scarf where the button should go on both sides.

6. Turn the pockets inside out. This will get them out of your way so you can attach the buttons. Stitch a button to each of the two spots you marked (see Tip). When you are done, secure the button with at least two or three knots. Turn the pockets back around. Now you're ready for cold weather!

TIP

When stitching on a button, go back and forth through the holes of the button a few times before tying a knot. When you are done, always double knot the thread. This will keep the buttons from getting loose or falling off as you use them.

Felt Pencil Case

Keep your pencils together and easy to find in this homemade case.

Materials

- Felt (18 x 3 inches, or 46 x 8 cm)
- Measuring tape
- Water-soluble marker
- Embroidery thread
- Embroidery needle (size 6)
- Button (make sure the needle fits through the holes of the button)
- Pins
- Scissors
- Pencils

Steps

1. Lay your fabric flat on a table. Measure 1 inch (2.5 cm) in from the short edge of the fabric. Then measure 1½ inches (4 cm) in from one of the long edges of the fabric. Mark it with your water-soluble marker.

2. Thread your needle and sew your button in this spot.

3. Turn the fabric over so the button is facing down. Measure 7 inches (18 cm) from the end that has the button on it and fold it back to this point. The button should now be facing up. Pin the fabric together.

4. Thread your needle and use an overcast stitch to join the edges of the pencil case together. When you get done with one side, tie and knot the thread. Do the same to the other side. Remove the pins.

5. Fold the top flap down on top of the button. Use the marker to mark exactly where the button is.

6. Use your scissors to cut a small, horizontal slit in the flap. The slit should be about the same size as the diameter of your button. Fold the flap closed and push the button through the slit. You are now ready to put your pencils in your case!

TIP
You can make a smaller version of this case to create a coin purse.

Finger Puppets

Make a bunny, a kitty, or a mouse.
Try making all three and putting on
a play with your new characters!

Materials

- Tape measure
- Water-soluble marker
- 1 sheet of gray felt (for the mouse)
- 1 sheet of pink felt (for all three creatures)
- 1 sheet of white felt (for the bunny)
- 1 sheet of yellow felt (for the kitty)
- Scissors
- Pins
- Cotton thread
- Sharp needle (size 4–6)
- Glue
- Googly eyes (optional)
- Fine-tip black permanent marker
- Small white pom-pom

Steps to make a mouse

1. Use your tape measure to mark a 2½ x 2-inch (6 x 5 cm) rectangle with the water-soluble marker on your gray piece of felt. Cut along the marked lines.
2. Fold the gray rectangle in half so you have a 1¼ x 2-inch (3 x 5 cm) rectangle. Pin it to keep it from moving.

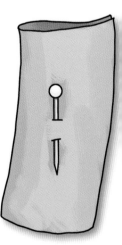

3. Thread your needle and sew along the long side of the rectangle using an overcast stitch. Remove the pins. This will be the mouse's body.

4. Mark and cut two small ears out of the gray felt for your mouse.

5. Mark and cut two pieces from the pink felt that are slightly smaller than the gray felt ears. These pieces will be the inside of your mouse's ears.

6. Use a running stitch to sew the pink felt to the gray felt. If the pieces are too small to stitch, you can glue them together.

7. Tuck the ears into the top of the mouse's body and pin them and the end of the felt tube shut.

8. Use a running stitch to stitch the ears to the top and to stitch the end of the body closed, all at the same time.

9. Glue the googly eyes to the front of your mouse or use the fine-tip marker to draw them.

10. Use the fine-tip marker to draw a nose and whiskers on your mouse's face.

11. Cut a small strip of gray felt approximately $1/8$ x $2 1/2$ inches (0.3 x 6 cm). This will be your mouse's tail. Stitch the tail to the back of your mouse.

Steps to make a bunny

1. Follow steps 1 through 10 of the mouse project. Use white felt instead of gray. Make the ears much longer than the mouse's ears.
2. Glue a white pom-pom to the back of your bunny for a tail.

Steps to make a kitty

1. Follow steps 1 through 10 of the mouse project. Use yellow felt instead of gray. Make pointy cat ears instead of round mouse ears.
2. Cut a small strip of yellow felt approximately 1/8 x 2 ½ inches (0.3 x 6 cm). This will be your kitty's tail. Stitch the tail to the back of your kitty.

TIP
You can create almost any animal you want to with this basic design. Simply change the felt colors and adjust the size and shape of the ears and tail!

Pillowcase

Snuggle up to this soft, cozy pillowcase when you need a break from sewing. This project requires a sewing machine and a hot iron, so ask an adult to help you.

Materials

- 1 piece of cotton fabric (27 x 36 inches, or 69 x 91 cm) for the main part of the pillowcase
- 1 piece of cotton fabric (9 x 36 inches, or 23 x 91 cm) for the cuff of the pillowcase
- 1 piece of cotton fabric (2 x 36 inches, or 5 x 91 cm) for piping
- Scissors
- Iron
- Pins
- Threaded sewing machine

Steps

1. Lay the three pieces of fabric on top of each other. Line them up along the edge where the fabric was folded on the **bolt**. Carefully cut the selvage edges from all three pieces of fabric. Selvage edges are the natural uncut edges of the fabric. They are woven so the fabric won't fray.

TIP
When you buy your fab look for cotton quilting fabric that is 36 inches (91 cm) wide. You can have the fabric store cu your fabric to the exact size you need. They have large tables and tools to make cutting straight lines very easy.

folded edge from bolt

selvage edge

23

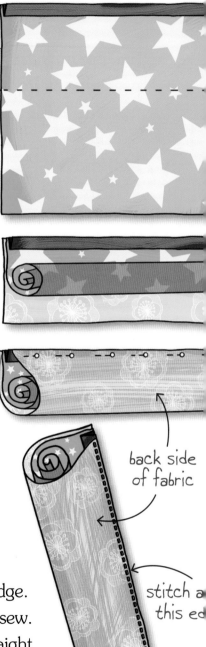

iron a crease

2. Fold the piping and cuff in half lengthwise. The right side of the fabric should be showing. With help from an adult, press the fold into the fabric with an iron.

3. Open up the pressed cuff and place it on the table with the right side of the fabric up. Place the main pillowcase fabric on top of it, lining it up along the top edge. This fabric should also be right side up. On top of that, place the pressed and still folded piping. The open end of the fold should line up with the top of the other fabrics under it.

4. Starting at the end where things are not lined up, roll the main part of the pillowcase. Continue rolling until you get about halfway into the cuff. Fold the cuff over the rolled main pillowcase and line the edge up with the other edges. Pin everything. When pinning, make sure all the fabric stays lined up.

5. Now you are ready to start sewing. Ask an adult to help you. Stitch along the pinned edge. Stay ¼ inch (0.6 cm) from the edge as you sew. Go slowly to make sure your seam stays straight. Remove the pins as you get to them.

back side of fabric

stitch a
this ed

fold over onto itself

6. Instead of tying knots with a sewing machine, you can sew backward for about half an inch and then forward again. Doing this a few times will secure the thread.

7. Once it is sewn, pull the rolled fabric out from the inside of the long sewn tube. Keep pulling until it all comes out. Once it is out, you should have your piping sewn to the cuff and main pillowcase with no seams showing. Lay it flat, right side up.

8. Fold it over onto itself and pin the edge and bottom of the case to secure it. Line up the cuff and piping as you do so. The pillowcase should be inside out now.

9. Go back to your sewing machine and sew along the edge. Stay ¼ inch (0.6 cm) from the edge as you go. Starting at the cuff, sew along the edge of the case.

back side of fabric

10. When you reach the bottom corner of the case, stop the machine with the needle in the down position, in the fabric. Lift up the machine's **presser foot** and turn the fabric so it is lined up to sew along the bottom.

11. Continue sewing along the bottom of the case. When you reach the end, secure the thread by going backward and forward with your stitching.

12. Turn your pillowcase right side out and put your pillow in it. Now you are ready for a good night's sleep!

Tooth Fairy Monster

When you lose a tooth, place it in the mouth of this pillow. Tie the pillow to the end of your bed. In the middle of the night, the tooth fairy will quietly take your tooth and replace it with money! Ask an adult to help you with the sewing machine and the iron.

Materials

- White felt (4 x 11 inches, or 10 x 28 cm)
- Water-soluble marker
- Scissors
- Tape measure
- Fabric (25 x 10 inches, or 64 x 25 cm)
- Iron
- Pins
- Threaded sewing machine
- 1 yard (91 cm) of thick ribbon
- Polyester stuffing
- Compass
- Embroidery thread
- Embroidery needle
- 2 buttons

Steps

1. Using the teeth pattern to the right, mark the white felt with the marker. Cut out your monster's teeth and set the piece aside.
2. Lay your fabric flat on the table, right side down. Fold 1 inch (2.5 cm) of fabric back from one of the 10-inch (25 cm) edges. With an adult's help, use an iron to press the fold into the fabric. This edge is the **hem**.

back side of fabric

3. Lay the fabric right side down with the hem edge at the top. Place the teeth on top of the folded hem edge, lining the bottom edge of the teeth with the bottom edge of the hem. Pin everything together.

4. Ask an adult to help you sew the teeth and hem into place.

5. Fold your ribbon in half and cut it along the fold. You should now have two 18-inch (46 cm) pieces.

6. Lay your fabric right side up on the table. Measure 11 inches (28 cm) down from the side that does not have the teeth and attach a ribbon to each edge of the fabric. Make sure the ribbon ends are lined up evenly with the fabric edges. Pin them in place. Fold the hanging ribbons loosely in the center of the fabric so they are not in the way of the edges.

7. Fold the side with the teeth down 4 inches (10 cm).

8. Fold the side that does not have the teeth up 10 inches (25 cm). This fold will be right behind where your ribbons are pinned.

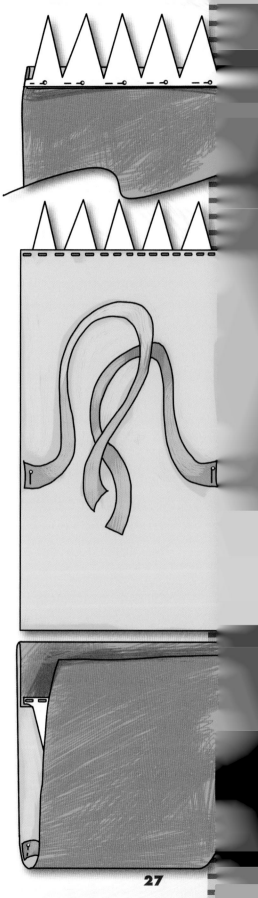

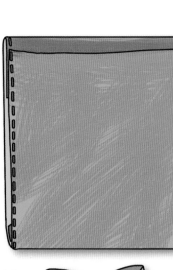

9. Pin each side together.

10. Use the sewing machine to sew each side. Stay ¼ inch (0.6 cm) from the edge as you sew. Make sure to sew the edge of the ribbon into the seam. Finish each side by going backward and forward with the machine. This will secure the seam.

11. Turn your pillow right side out through the fold.

12. Stuff your pillow with polyester stuffing. Make sure to push the stuffing deep into the corners.

13. Use the compass to draw two circles on the white felt. They should each have a diameter of about 2 inches (5 cm). Cut them out. These are your tooth fairy monster's eyes.

14. If marks show up from your compass, turn your circle over so the marks do not show. Put buttons in the center of each of the white circles and stitch the buttons in place. Be sure to tie a few knots to secure the buttons.

15. Place the circles on the top corners of your pillow. Pin the circles in place.

16. Thread your needle and sew the eyes in place with an overcast stitch. Knot the end when you get all the way around each circle. Remove the pins. You are now ready to hang your pillow at the end of your bed!

Sew Creative!

Sewing is a skill that you can use the rest of your life. You can use it to mend your favorite pair of jeans or to design a dress. Many people make a living sewing. Others sew just for fun.

The number of things you can make by sewing is limited only by your imagination. Inspiration can come from things you see around you. Search the Internet for ideas. Keep a sketchbook of your ideas. Draw in it whenever you see something that inspires you. Make notes on the sides of your drawings so that you remember what you were thinking.

"Sew," get creative!

What will you sew next?

Glossary

bolt (BOHLT) a roll of cloth

diameter (dye-AM-i-tur) a straight line through the center of a circle, connecting opposite sides

garments (GAHR-muhnts) pieces of clothing

hem (HEM) an edge of material that has been folded over and sewn down

mass-produce (MASS pruh-DOOS) make large amounts of identical things with machines in a factory

patented (PAT-uhn-tid) obtained legal documents giving the inventor of an item the sole rights to manufacture or sell it

presser foot (PREH-sur FOOT) the flat metal piece on a sewing machine that holds material flat as the needle pokes through

tailors (TAY-lurz) people who make or alter clothes

textile (TEK-stile) woven or knitted fabric or cloth

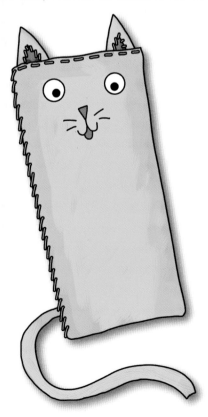

For More Information

Books

Bull, Jane. *Made by Me*. New York: DK Publishing, 2009.

Kerr, Sophie. *A Kid's Guide to Sewing: Learn to Sew with Sophie and Her Friends*. Lafayette, CA: C&T Publishing, 2013.

Wrigley, Annabel. *We Love To Sew*. Lafayette, CA: C&T Publishing, 2014.

Web Sites

Not So Idle Hands—15 Easy Sewing Projects for Kids, Tweens, & Teens

http://notsoidlehands.com/2014/01/15-easy-sewing-projects-for-kids-tweens-and-teens.html

This Web site offers a range of sewing ideas. Some projects are more difficult than others.

Skip to My Lou—Get Kids Sewing Series

www.skiptomylou.org/get-kids-sewing-series

Take a look at this Web site for some more simple sewing projects to try.

Index

About the Author

Kathleen Petelinsek is a children's book illustrator, writer, and designer. As a child, she spent her summers drawing and painting. She still loves to do the same today, but now all her work is done on the computer. When she isn't working on her computer, she can be found outside swimming, biking, running, or playing in the snow of southern Minnesota.